THE WEIGHT OF THE WORLD

Connie C. Tomlin-Vogt
THE WEIGHT OF THE WORLD

—

Published by - Spines
ISBN: 979-8-89691-488-4

THE WEIGHT OF THE WORLD

CONNIE C. TOMLIN-VOGT

Dedication Letter

I am dedicating my work to my husband, children, grandchildren, and grandparents, who have been there through thick and thin. Things got hard at times if it was not for their shoulders to lean on. I do not know what I would have done. They were the only ones that I could talk with to ease my heart and mind. We will always be as one because "WE ARE ONE". **CCTV**

Contents

Introduction
The Weight of the World

The WEIGHT OF THE WORLD reminds us that there are things that have transpired and occurred to some that should never be experienced by anyone. You are only ugly when you take from the ones who really need it the most. Maybe if you wear a paper suit it will do just fine for a few, because the talking and hatred never stops. We all know what assumption does to us. Be satisfied for who you are made of, the good things that are there. The wants and worries will go away and all of your needs certainly do come. ***CCTV***

BOOK 1

FAITH IS A CHOICE

A Message To My Readers

To my Readers Faith Is A Choice that I will take for the good and not the bad. When things are not going the way they should Faith is what you can count on. The Faith within Jesus Christ and yourself will make each one of us a person you can believe in. Prayer also helps soothe the soul from being confused and takes away a lot of hurt, anger and pain. Finding a pathway to Heaven instead of Hell Faith guides us into another world. ***CCTV***

A KINGDOM CITIZEN

I am A Kingdom Citizen

From the World of

Holy Heaven

Come to my Town

To share my Joy

For Laws are filled with Love

And the Government is full of

The Holy Spirit

Come to earn your Citizenship

At the best Kingdom of all

Listen to hear your name call

A LITTLE CHILD'S PRAYER

The time has come

For us to say

A Little Child's Prayer

Praying to you

GOD

To just hold us near

Keeping you in

Our hearts and minds

You will lead us there

Knowing that you

Have kept us

Safe from any harm

Oh Heavenly Father

You are so dear

You gave your son

JESUS CHRIST

Who is everywhere, AMEN?

A MIRACLE

Is there A Miracle that will make us all new?

Will it come at the first of dawn?

Is there A Miracle that will make us all new?

Will it come during the morning dew?

Is there A Miracle that will make us all new?

Will it come in the afternoon for a few?

Is there A Miracle that will make us all new?

Will it come in the bright evening sun?

Is there A Miracle that will make us all new?

Will it come at the time of dust without a fuss?

Is there A Miracle that will make us all new?

Will it come in the night when we sleep tight?

If every heart has joyfulness in it

Connie C. Tomlin-Vogt

Let the love of JESUS CHRIST exist

On Earth as it is in Heaven

Keeping the Faith in Him

Miracles will come all day long.

Connie C. Tomlin-Vogt

A PRAYER TO MY LORD

LORD,

Keep our hearts and mind

From being so confused

LORD,

Hear my prayers

Humans are not perfect

Every breath we take

Is very much a sin

The love that you share

Will never end

It comes repeatedly again

LORD,

Your love makes a happy home

From the blood you have shed

Brings love in the hearts

Of all who do not understand

Send us blessings from Heaven

To guard our doors below

For man do not know

LORD,

We place our hands in yours

For guidance to the Promised Land

The Faith we have in you

Keeps us holding your hand

While we take our stand

Thank you,

LORD,

For carrying us through

From the old and to the new

AMEN and AMEN

A SMILE

Put on A Smile, not a frown

Lay your weapons down

To the ground

Put on A Smile, not a frown

Enough blood has been shed

What is moving inside of your head?

Put on A Smile, not a frown

Taking a life, you cannot give

Is against the Holy Bible

Also, against Christ's will

Put on A Smile, not a frown

When his Kingdom comes to Earth

Without Faith, all the sinners

Should be on trial first

A SOLDIER

A Soldier that put

The little ones to bed

While they rest

Their pretty little heads

On call to fight a war

With someone

He does not know

Pacing the floors

From the windows

To the doors

Not knowing

Which way shall they go?

Two hours away

So, they will not be delayed

To get on an airplane

Too, make this world

Have tremendous days

Let there be peace

Instead of war

Therefore, our children can

Play together forevermore

AMERICANS, AMERICANS

Americans, Americans

It is time to let

By gone be by gone

Putting the past behind us

Heals old wounds

Asking for forgiveness

When wrong is done

Clears our conscience

Moreover, help us to move on

Americans, Americans

Let there be between each other

Peace, love, shelter

And to share a piece of bread

With one another

Americans, Americans

Others are knocking at our doors

Taking care of our own homeland

Is what keeps us a flow

Put destruction and hate

On the other side of the gate

Americans, Americans

Stop stabbing each other

In the back

Because their shoes or clothes match

Be faithful unto JESUS

He will guide you through

And have a beautiful white robe

That will make us all new

DOES IT MATTER

Why is racism so wrong for us all?

Why the human mind is not strong?

Why when it is mention?

Why is there such great tension?

Why does color really matters?

Why does it batter when we hear chatters?

Why does glass shatter?

I wish I may,

With all our might

GOD loves everyone

Who is in or out

Of his sight

FAITH

The Faith we have in JESUS

A road that we must travel

To make it into Heaven

We must walk through

The heavenly types of weather

The Faith we have in JESUS

Are ladders we must climb

To make it into Heaven

We face obstacles each time

The Faith we have in JESUS

Each footstep we should take

To make it into Heaven

We must first

Knock on Heaven's Gate

The Faith we have in JESUS

A Cross-which we must carry

Connie C. Tomlin-Vogt

To make it into Heaven

Our Faith, it will lead us there

FATHER

FATHER,

Please hear my prayer

Lead us on those weary roads

Where traveling has no end

Guide us on this scary path

For you have never compared

With your open arms

Therefore, we will not be scared

FATHER,

We love you, and we are not afraid

Please hear my prayer

Forgive those

Who put you last in line

Without letting your light shine

FATHER,

Bless them

When the lines are long

And the glass doors

Are slammed in our face

We know that you have

Us a better place

FATHER,

We want you to stay

In our hearts, every day

You come first in every way

That is what makes us pray

FATHER,

You are above all others

We put our faith in you

Before and after one another, AMEN

FIGHTING FOR LIFE

To the little fighters

Since the day they were born

Fighting For Life, asking JESUS

Not to take them home

Some days were at its worst

And some days were at its best

Having Faith in the results

From the test

You are growing

Stronger and stronger

Day by day

Hoping our LORD and SAVIOR

Is hearing us pray

The strength that you are given

Is all so amazing

Keep up the good work

At Fighting For Life

It will help us all

Sleep throughout the night

Connie C. Tomlin-Vogt

To know that you have

Fought for your life

During a tough fight

CONNIE C. TOMLIN-VOGT

FIGHTING FOR THE CHILDREN

Fighting For The Children

Is a charm

It keeps them safe

From violence and crime

Guns are carried

By our children

Actions are taken

So, be careful

Do what it takes

For Heaven sake

This is a hard

To win battle

Our Faith in you, LORD

Helps us hold

Down this clatter

FORGIVE THE UNFORGIVABLE

Forgive The Unforgivable

Who have these idol Gods

And put them before you

Our FATHER GOD and your son

CHRIST, our SAVIOR LORD

Forgive The Unforgivable

Who makes false images of things

Here on Earth that, we can see

Forgive The Unforgivable

For those who take

The LORD thy GOD Holy name in vain

Forgive The Unforgivable

Who work for more than six days

Forgive the Unforgivable

Who does not keep the seventh day

For rest and worship

Forgive The Unforgivable

Who disobey their Mother and Father

For they have to shorten

Their days on this land

Forgive The Unforgivable

Who kills and cannot give life

Forgive The Unforgivable

Who commits adultery upon their Spouse

Forgive The Unforgivable

Who steal and are considered as thieves

Forgive The Unforgivable

Who covers the neighbor's house

Or anything that belongs

To the neighbor

FORWARD

Put your best foot Forward

You will achieve

Make sure you do not encounter

Any of those thieves

Put your best foot Forward

You will succeed

Keep an open mind

To help you believe

Put your best foot Forward

You will be relieved

Therefore, you do not

Have to ask

Anyone for your needs

Put your best foot Forward

And you have planted your seed

While making plans

For the right deal

GOD HAS

GOD,

Has no color in his sight

GOD,

Has the color of pure light

GOD,

Has love with no hate

GOD,

Just want us to know

It is not too late

Please be kind

So, that

Everyone,

Will live and have

A peace of mind

GOD'S LIGHT

The darkness of the night

Is the way

To the great light

We should always

Keeps it burning bright

Doing it GOD'S way

Will make it all right

So, please make sure

Everything done is in sight

And help those persons

Who are willing

To put up a tough fight

When seeking GOD'S LIGHT

GOD'S POWER

The power of GOD

Will twist and turn

And make you think

That you are going to bend

The power of GOD

Will make you

Shake and shiver

To let you know

You should be a giver

The power of GOD

Will make your

Mourn and groan

To let you know

You maybe scorn

The power of GOD

Will make you

Dance and shout

To let you see

That he is on your route

GOD'S POWER heals with FAITH

The only thing

He wants us to do

Is to participate

GOD'S POWER

HAVE IT BAD

The person,

Who thinks they Have It Bad

What that person wants to know

Is what makes them sad

Not knowing if they

Will ever find out

Because no one

Will open their mouth

Living a lie

Is not where they want to be

Being honest

Is how you retrieve

Start living the good life

Stop living in greed

Keep honesty

And love in your heart

Faith will lead you to thee

HEAVENLY FATHER

Oh, Holy,

Righteous Heavenly Father

Once again

I come before thee

With an open heart

Also open mind

Asking you time

And time again

To keep

Your blessings upon

This sinful world

Father,

You know my heart

As well as my mind

You put strength

In this old temple of mines

When I am weak and weary

With a blank mind

The knowledge you give

Connie C. Tomlin-Vogt

I will forever share

To all that cares

Every step I take

There is not enough to make

Please let me walk

Without looking

Over my shoulders

Let us walk side by side

And pace for pace

Heavenly Father

This is not a race, AMEN

HEAVY LOAD

After starting

All over again

The happiness

That has sat beyond

Has washed away

All of my sins

I am feeling

Whole again

It has been

So amazing

The heavy load

I have carried

With such enormous Faith

Uplifting my heart

That I may not be afraid

I cannot be afraid

Of that Heavy Load

It will not

Take over me again

HUGO

HUGO came

We wanted to ride out the storm

But suddenly realized

We should be heading towards home

Under shelter as safe as could be

The hurricane sounding

Like a moving freight train

Coming close, but with flying debris

The eye of the storm came

Just as silent as can be

Changing of colors in the sky

With the smell

Of fresh flowers in the air

JESUS CHRIST was right there

The back of the storm

It made us pray

A little harder

Without even a bother

Hoping that his work

Would soon be over

Waiting and watching

For morning to come

Awake to a new day

To see what our LORD has done

Thanking him for a miracle

Those lives were saved

Therefore, we rejoiced

While singing with praise

I KNOW

I know,

There is a GOD,

That is living

In heaven

I Know,

It will be

A rough road to cross

Those we must bear

I Know,

To keep Love

In my heart

Without any despair

I Know there is a

GOD,

In Heaven somewhere

I cannot wait

To meet him right there

I WANT TO BE LIKE JESUS

I Want To Be Like JESUS

He is the one

Who will please us

I Want To Be Like JESUS

He is the one

That will not tease us

I Want To Be Like JESUS

He is the one

Who will feed us

I Want To Be Like JESUS

He is the one

Who sees us

I Want To Be Like JESUS

He is the one

Who needs us

I Want To Be Like JESUS

He is the one

Who will guide

And lead us

I WANT TO BE LIKE JESUS

IS THERE

Is There a right and a wrong?

Is There a weak and a strong?

Is There a big and a small?

Is There a sweet and a sour?

Is There an up and a down?

Is There a front and a back?

Is There a shout and a whisper?

Is There a ride and a walk?

Is There war without any peace?

Whatever it is

Take it to our LORD

Leave it there

At your own

Faith and Will

Praying will get us there

KEEP ON STRUGGLING

The size Tiny as an ink dot

The size is as small as a toy building block

The size is Medium as a floor grandfather's clock

The size Large as a mountainside granite rock,

KEEP ON STRUGGLING

Because the ladder is long

The ocean is wide and deep

We do not have to weep

Keeping the FAITH

Will not let us

Lose our fate

KEEP ON WALKING

Keep On Walking

To the kingdom

That Promised Land

Keep On Walking

To the kingdom

Too, take your stand

Keep On Walking

To the kingdom

Too, shake Christ's hand

Keep On Walking

To the kingdom

Because the Devil will try

Too, make other plans

Keep On Walking

To The Kingdom

CONNIE C. TOMLIN-VOGT

That Promised Land

Connie C. Tomlin-Vogt

KEEPING THE FAITH

You want me

To fall on my face

I am KEEPING THE FAITH

And staying in the race

One day, my race will be won

Soon, you will see

I have overcome

To make the right decisions

I have invested in myself

The FAITH I have

Is timing me through the test

Earth is a rat race

That no one has alternatively

Never going to win

I will take my rest

In your Heavenly home

With positive thinking

I will then rise

When Judgment Day comes

I cannot back slide

I am human too

KINGDOM BUILDING

I am building

My KINGDOM up to HEAVEN

No one can stop me

My LORD and I

Are at a perfect state

My MASTER, he is so loyal

The FAITH in him

Keeps me at a boil

With trust and desire

The LOVE I have for him

Is Hot as fire

You are the HOLY MASTER

The one that I will follow

While doing my

Kingdom Building

Up to my Glorious MASTER

LET HIM IN

Let the,

"LORD JESUS CHRIST"

Come into your heart

You will find yourself

To be a better person

He will make a way

Out of no way

When no one is around

Do not call on his name

In the time of need

Call on it at all times

You will receive

Bad things do happen

To all mankind

JESUS

Is willing to forgive

So Let Him In

Let Him In

OH MASTER

MASTER, OH MASTER,

You are thou, LORD JESUS,

I am calling

On your name, JESUS

You are sending me

So many signs

In ways that

I would never

Imagine LORD

Your signs

Are the wonderful

And the marvelous

MASTER

There are times

When my mind

Have all the doubts SAVIOR

The FAITH I have

In my HEART

Has overpowered my mind

For you CHRIST

This is the only thing

That has kept me on time

Is the Faith within myself

Pretending is like

Breaking up all ties

For being the REDEEMER

Be yourself

Do not worry about anyone

Other than yourself

ONE HALF

Half Black

Half White

We are all

GODS' children

Under his light

Half Black

Half White

We can trust GOD

With all our might

Half Black

Half White

We are all the same

In GOD's sight

Half Black

Half White

We all should say

Everything will be all right

No questions ask

If you are

ONE HALF Black, Black or White

Color should not matter

In no one's' sight

Everyone should have

The same rights

ONE NIGHT WITH THE KING

One Night With The KING

Oh, how will I sing

Until the morning bells ring

One Night With The KING

One Night With The KING

I will call all to join in

To sing his praise

One Night With The KING

One Night With The KING

There will be a feast

For all who come to greet

And sit at his feet

On that night with the KING

One Night With The KING

One Night With The KING

All will rejoice by laughter

While celebrating

The morning after

One Night With The KING

Rejoicing now and then

ONE NIGHT WITH THE KING

PEACE

P is for the Peace, it should be all over the world.

E is for the Equality of every proud boy and girl.

A is for the Accountability that is due to and from.

C is for the Caring between those that we meet.

E is for the Earth we share as a treat

When PEACE is on

This green Earth

GODS' LOVE will have conquered

Every believer's HEART

Without all kinds of sound

Throughout this world

Blessing all Boys and Girls

PLEASE YOU

Is there anything

That will ever

PLEASE YOU

Be happy

For the good things

That you have

And let go

Of the bad things

That will try

To make you go mad

If for any reason

In any season

You are not, please

PRAY to GOD

While you fall

On your knees

Connie C. Tomlin-Vogt

RED BIRD

Red Bird, Red Bird

I Love You

Let the blood of JESUS

Rain down on you

Including the whole world, too

From the pine needles below

To the tree branches above

The nest that you have build

It has revealed to us

There is still time

For his Love to share

With a Heart that forgives

To let him come in

He will wash away

All of our sins

To make every one of us

Completely again

SKY ANGLES

Sky Angles,

You are my eyes

From the Heavens up above

Please catch me

When I am about to fall

Sky Angles,

You are my eyes

From the Heavens up above

Help to put love in my heart

That makes me feel tall

Sky Angles,

You are my eyes

From the Heavens up above

Ease my mind

When I hear your call

Sky Angles,

Connie C. Tomlin-Vogt

You are my eyes

From the Heavens up above

I am waiting to take my place

In GOD'S Heavenly Stall

We, Will Party At The Grand Ball

SOME PEOPLE

Some People

Make you happy

Some People

Make you glad

Some People

Make you snappy

Some People

Make you sad

Some People

Just do not even care

Put your trust in

JESUS,

He will,

Pull you through

Connie C. Tomlin-Vogt

With all the love

That he has

Waiting for you

72

SPOKEN KNOWLEDGE

Spoken Knowledge,

It took GOD six days

To create the Heaven and Earth

Spoken Knowledge,

The Sabbath day was prepared

For rest and worship

Spoken Knowledge,

GOD made Adam the male

From a pile of dirt

Spoken Knowledge,

GOD made Eve from Adam's ribcage

Both blind with a blank mind

Spoken Knowledge,

Adam and Eve

Lived in the Garden of Eden

With many fruitful trees

One apple tree

Forbidden by GOD

Which they should not eat

Spoken Knowledge,

The forbidden apples they ate

Adam and Eve's eyes became open

They began to cover themselves

With fig leaves

Spoken Knowledge,

On GOD'S return to the Garden of Eden

Adam and Eve

Hiding behind shrubs and bushes

Furthermore, this is what began

Our world, too, sin

STARTING WITH ME

Starting With Me

A change you will see

A change that is due for you and me

Something we both

Should look forward to heal

In this lifetime so, let it be

Starting With Me

A change you will see

A change that is due for you and me

LORD gives us the strength

Do not let the Devil's willpower be

Starting With Me

A change you will see

A change that is due

For you and me

With FAITH in our Hearts

We will be safe so let it be

Starting With Me

A change you will see

A change that is due

For you and me

We all should sacrifice

To let the Love be

Starting With Me

A change you will see

A change that is due

For you and me

Be happy when the rainfalls

The sun will shine

We cannot stop it, so let it be

STICKING IT OUT

Sticking It Out

Through thick and thin

GOD will be there

Until the end

Pray each and every day

Our sins will

Be washed away

Put your hands

In his hands

He will make you

A better man

Sticking It Out

You can, and I can

THE BIG MAN

The BIG MAN upstairs

Sitting in his golden chair

Waiting and watching

The old and new

Hoping he can make

Everyone's wishes

And dreams come true

Accepting things

As they come

Ask him with praise

And forgiveness

He will see you through

The Pearly Gates

Will open wide that we

May enter through

CONNIE C. TOMLIN-VOGT

THE BODY OF CHRIST

To all believers

We are The Body Of CHRIST

Living in his body

Is like living in a shell

Being as one

We are equal to none

To all believers

We are The Body Of CHRIST

In order to enter

You must pay the price

All who are living shall die

Every one of us

Have told a lie

To all believers

We are The Body Of CHRIST

It does not matter

If your skin color is

Connie C. Tomlin-Vogt

Red, purple, blue, or yellow

To all believers

We are The Body Of CHRIST

He makes no mistake about it

He punishes those who think

They can do without him

We are THE BODY OF CHRIST

THIS LITTLE TOWN

In This Little Town

Seen some old faces

From back in the days

Looking like bums

Not caring if GOD

Is going to come

No sorrow or forsaken

All wants to be

In creation

Churning and burning

With every might

Trying to destroy

Everyone thinks that insight

GOD, please

Put a shine on this

And Every Little Town

So that everyone

Will be able to wear

Their diamond crown

Connie C. Tomlin-Vogt

TOO MY MASTER

I am getting stronger

As the days go by

I can feel it

Within the strength of what

My LORD has given me

I must keep pushing myself

And telling myself

Those things are better

Hoping they will get

Even healthier

As time goes on

Being in a rush

Can cause total chaos

This is why

I thank my SAVIOR

From morning, noon and night

Till thereafter

I am still praying

TOO MY MASTER

It is also something

Man cannot take

Are my prayers

Too My,

BENEVOLENCE MASTER

That I make

It is also something

Man cannot take

Are my prayers

Too My,

BENEVOLENCE MASTER

That I make

TODAY

Today,

I will kneel

On my knees to pray

Today,

I will try

To help someone

Along the way

Today,

I am the same person

From yesterday

Today,

I will not change

For tomorrow is just

A different day

Today,

I will make sure

That everything stays the same

When there is a change

And to play no games

For JESUS CHRIST

Is his Holy and Righteous name

TRY

We can make it

If we Try

Do not sit

And start to cry

Try to reach

For the stars

In the sky

Remember I told

You to Try

Always Try

It will give

You such pride

Keep your head

Held up high

Also, remember

I told you

Too, Try with a stride

Our SAVIOR

Is who keeps us alive

UNDER THE SPOUT

Under The Spout

Where the glory comes out

Will make everyone

Scream and shout

There is no doubt

Under The Spout

Where the glory comes out

Our love grows forever more

Love will be for all to feel

Under The Spout

Where the glory comes out

The Devil will throw a rock

Stalk when there is no knock

Please do not let him

Watch your clock

Under The Spout

Where the glory comes out

FAITH will guide us

For what comes out of the mouth

88

Under The Spout

Where the glory comes out

JESUS is our SAVIOR

He nurtures you from a Sprout

WALKING IN VICTORY

Who will be

Walking In Victory

That we will meet

It is for certain

All in the world

Will be seen

Who will be

Walking In Victory

That we will meet

I hope for sure

It will be you and me

Who will be

Walking In Victory

That we will meet

Through the love

From his heart

The parade is free

Who will be

Walking In Victory

That we will meet

To all believers'

He will most definitely seek

Who will be

Walking In Victory

That we will meet

The ones with FAITH

He will welcome

Without any defeat

Walking In Victory

Is where we will meet

WANT

GOD,

Want you to put

JESUS

In your life

GOD is our FATHER

JESUS is HIS SON

We are GOD'S children

Trying too

Make it home

JESUS our BROTHER

Leading us through

This raging storm

Serve him faithfully

And the Holy Spirit

Blessings will come

WHO JESUS IS

I want to know Who JESUS Is

He is the one

Still giving us bread

I want to know Who JESUS Is

He is the one

Who will heal us

When we are sick in bed

I want to know Who JESUS Is

He is the one

Who clothes us

When we do not have a thread

I want to know Who JESUS Is

He is our

LORD and SAVIOR

Who is not dead

But very much alive

Connie C. Tomlin-Vogt

Waiting for our souls

Once we enter on High

YOU CAN

You Can,

Hear what you want to hear

You Can,

See what you want to see

You Can,

Smell whatever is in the air

That sends off a smell

You Can,

Touch when there is something to touch

You Can,

Taste whatever it is to taste

You Can,

Do what any man can do

Stop doubting yourself

And JESUS will guide

You through the test

Summary

Faith Is A Choice that lives within each one of us. It captures our Heart, Mind and Body to a complete guidance of Prayers. Having this Faith helps keep the Heart at ease without any aches and pain. The Faith in our Mind is in the Clouds to keep the evilness out in the open. The Faith in our Body also has all the control of a spirit that is unbelievable. With this belief and understanding of how delicate a Prayer works when it is repeated silently or out loud. Faith will lift the SOUL into a height of greatness and rewards. Faith Is A Choice to show we are capable of doing whatever it takes to seek Faith in Jesus Christ. Faith will guide us into this unknown world of pleasure that no one could ever dream. When things are not going the way they should. Take one-half of a second to call on the Master's name. He has all the answers for the questions that we may inquire about. The relief that Prayer brings when calling on his name also endures a gift of giving that is so delightful to all men for their own sake. CCTV

BOOK 2

LOVE AND HATE THIS LIFE

A Message To My Readers

To my readers, Love And Hate This Life sometimes love and hate will make you laugh, and then it will make you cry. Take the love and share it, take the hate and bury it. Listening to what others are talking about when they are in need of an ear. Give a positive response to show our Love is forever there. Love will take over the heart and the mind with any pleasant gesture. Keep the love growing stronger, it will last longer, and hate will not exist anymore. ***CCTV***

A GOOD MAN

A Good Man cannot be

That is hard to find

Look for the ones

That has a dime

Who cares about time

Listening to the wind chimes

Everything will be just fine

Tell him you will

Always be mines

This is what makes

A good man shine

A FRIEND IS...

What A Friend Is?

Someone you can count on

Through thick and thin

Someone who will be there

Until the day has ended

Someone who makes you laugh

Instead of cry

Someone who will make

You happy

When you are sad

Someone who is hoping
You will never die

Someone who will make

You are happy when you sad

Someone who does not want

To see you leave

Because it makes them mad

Someone who will keep

Your spirits are soaring high

Someone who do not want

To say good-bye

This is A Friend

Who says

I can be A Friend and

A Friend I am

A MOTHER

A Mother

Is love

Instead of hate

A Mother

Is someone

Who is fair

An also cares

A Mother

Is willing to admit

Her wrongs

To show that she

Is very strong

These are three standards

Of what a Mother

Should be

Thank you

Mothers and children

Let us get

Closer to thee

ACCEPT ME

Accept Me

For whom I am

Or don't accept

Me at all

Don't try to find

The little things

That doesn't matter

Just let me be me

Not who you

Want me to be

Because you are no one

To judge

Anything about me

Accept me

And let me be me

AFRAID

Afraid to feel

The way you want to feel

Afraid to say

The things you want to say

Afraid to do

The things you want to do

Afraid to be

The person you want to be

Afraid is just

Another word

Swimming around

Inside our heads

There are no reasons

For you to be Afraid

Be happy instead of Afraid

ALL ABOUT

Meeting new people

Is what

It's All About

Talking and laughing

Shows you can do

With or without

Some people we meet

Say hello

By nodding with a speak

Others look at you

Like their hands

In the place

Of their feet

You see their heads

Are filled with air

Misery is what

They fear

Connie C. Tomlin-Vogt

ALWAYS ON MY MIND

You are always on my mind

When the wind blow

Even when the planes fly

And even when the dust rise

You are always on my mind

You are always on my mind

When the lights shine

Even when a baby cries

And even when I say good-bye

You are always on my mind

You are always on my mind

In my heart

Even in my sleep

And even when

I am about to eat

My Love is forever deep

Connie C. Tomlin-Vogt

You are Always On My Mind

Always On My Mind

ANGRY

Being Angry

Does not solve

Anyone's problems

The calmness

One show

Tells how

Intelligent one is

Being upset

Not giving or taking

Whatever one does

Is at one's

Own risk

Settle down

On the right road

To town

Stop looking

Like a clown

BENEATH

Beneath

The one you love

Like a baseball hiding

In a baseball glove

Will it ever be Love

On the inside or outside

Of a baseball glove

When the ball is tossed

It is time to forgive

Therefore, we all

Can come together

With kisses

Hugs and cheers

Never be Beneath

The one you Love

BLACK HAWK'S DOWN 2001

Black Hawk's Down 2001

United States Peacekeepers

Went to save and rescue

Part of a Country

That was called a town

We love you, men

Who have fought

On hostile grounds

For the bravest

Who have died

And the bravest

Who have lived

We love you

With kindness

For being sincere

We are proud of you

Our Soldiers

We Love you so dear

To have helped someone

Connie C. Tomlin-Vogt

Through a Civil War

From those murders

And thieves they fear

That carried weapons

Known as guns that killed

Children, women and men

DANGEROUS GAMES

Nuclear Wars

Are Dangerous Games

Playing in fire

Is a sin and a shame

Nuclear Wars

A step from HELL

To see that old Devil

We are living

In his sell

STOP Nuclear Wars

Where all

Can live together

To make each other

Extremely HAPPIER

Forever and Ever

Dangerous Games

Should be Never

Connie C. Tomlin-Vogt

FACE THE NATION

Face The Nation

Will make you a better man

Face The Nation

Stop making these secret plans

Face The Nation

Play by the rules

Face The Nation

Do not be so cruel

Face The Nation

Speak up when

You have good news

Face The Nation

It should be

Equal for all men

Stop making up excuses

About the stroke of a pen

Things do show

How manly you are

Cowards only stand

Behind closed doors

FEELINGS

Is it right to hurt

Someone's feelings

But your feelings

Are too good to be hurt

It Is like

Putting your face

In a pile of dirt

Everyone should take

Other's feelings

Under consideration

If one link of a chain

Could rattle by itself

No one would need any help

Ugly words cause confusion

Who knows what will happen next

When feelings have been hurt

Trying to make the next man feel

Like he is not wearing

A pair of pants or a shirt

CONNIE C. TOMLIN-VOGT

Feelings should come first

Connie C. Tomlin-Vogt

FORGETTING

Adults,

Keep Forgetting

They were children, too

Now, put yourself

In a child's shoe

Abusing and killing our children

Does not accomplish anything

It makes issues worst

That should let us know

We need to take a rest

Let our children know

Who is the adult

And who is the child

Children will test you

Not meaning any harm

Showing them you love them

Shows you have a charm

Adults, please do not forget

We were children, too

That will make our children happy

And they will know what to do

Connie C. Tomlin-Vogt

GRANDMOTHERS WE NEED YOU

Grandmothers,

We need you

To get these children told

To let them know

They are not running the show

Grandmothers,

We need you

To get these children told

To let them know

That listening is the way to go

Grandmothers,

We need you

To get these children told

To let them know

Doing the right thing

Will make their pockets grow

Grandmothers,

We need you

To get these children told

To let them know

Guns and violence

Are not the roads to take

Death between our children

Is a pattern

We should not make

Being each other's friend

Is the path we should not fake

HAPPINESS IS...

Happiness Is...

The way life should go

Being happy is how we grow

Happiness Is...

The way life should go

Being happy is all I know

Happiness Is...

The way life should go

Being happy is what will show

Happiness is...

The way life should go

Being happy is to let

The negative things take a blow

Happiness Is...

The way life should go

Being happy will

Keep you with the flow

HEARTS OF STONE

Hearts Of Stone

Is not the way

I want to go home

Hearts Of Stone

Loving is what you need

To keep you strong

Hearts Of Stone

Keeping the magic

Will keep you

Safe from harm

Hearts Of Stone

We will laugh and cry

When the old times are gone

Hearts Of Stone

Stand by

Each other's side

To keep us

From being torn

You do not have

A Heart Of Stone

Connie C. Tomlin-Vogt

HOW SOUND

How Sound,

Do you think

I am

How Sound,

If I

Do understand

How Sound,

Will it make me

A better man

How Sound,

Because I know

That, I can

How sound,

This is what makes us

All human

CONNIE C. TOMLIN-VOGT

HUMANS DON'T UNDERSTAND

I don't have a place to lay my head

Life is like a jigsaw puzzle

With thousands of pieces

It takes a lifetime to put together

Still, Humans Don't Understand

I don't have a place to lay my head

To keep putting the jigsaw puzzle

Together, over and over again

There has to be an end

Still, Humans Don't Understand

I don't have a place to lay my head

The humans who pretend

Like they do not understand

Hurt the pockets

Of every man they can

Still, Humans Don't Understand

I don't have a place to lay my head

Individuals try

To control others' life

This takes away from a man

Being a man

Still, Humans Don't Understand

I don't have a place to lay my head

Making laws with doubt

If someone they love are caught

Mortal pretend

They do not understand

GOD is there

You will answer to his command

Still, Humans Don't Understand

HURT AND PAIN

When there is

Hurt And Pain

It is like taking

Two steps backwards

Because the heart

Has been rearrange

Satisfying

Someone else's needs

Will not

Make you believe

That the heart

Is as gentle

As a seed

If there is

Hurt And Pain

The heart feels

Like it is about

To bleed like rain

Why does the heart

Connie C. Tomlin-Vogt

Gives off

So much pain

All it needs is love

Instead of

Hurt And Pain

I – N – G LOVE

A Husband and Wife

are teams of one

Helping each other

Through a terrible storm

Standing by

Each other's side

Day and night

Keeping the home fire

Burning bright

Making sure

Those things are right

Showing each other

They will be there forever

LOV-I-N-G

CAR-I-N-G

SHAR-I-N-G

Is what keeps

The marriage together

As it wears

Connie C. Tomlin-Vogt

And tears for ever

INSANE

All the

Hurt, anger and pain

Should we all be Insane?

Attempting to keep things

Held down tight

Struggling to make it right

Knowing that this

Is not a perfect world

Praying we will not

All go to hell

That is why

We all must be tame

Unless we are all

Going Insane

This will be a sin

And shame for all

To go Insane

Connie C. Tomlin-Vogt

LAY HIS HEAD

Every man

Should have a place

To Lay His Head

Even when he does not

Have a piece of bread

Every man

Should have a place

To Lay His Head

Even when there is no

Work ahead

Every man

Should have a place

To Lay His Head

Even when the electric

Is dead

Every man

Should have a place

To Lay His Head

Even when his body

Is as cold as lead

Every man

Should have a place

To Lay His Head

Connie C. Tomlin-Vogt

LET ME BE ME

By the expression on my face

Why can't you Let Me Be Me

By the way, I stare

Why can't you Let Me Be Me

By the style, I fix my hair

Why can't you Let Me Be Me

By the clothes I wear

Why can't you Let Me Be Me

By the shoes, I put on my feet

Why can't you Let Me Be Me

By the car, I drive

Why can't you Let Me Be Me

By the home, I live in

Why can't you Let Me Be Me

Why can't you Let Me Be Me

Because you want to be like me

Or do you want to be me

Just Let Me Be Me

Not who you or anyone else

Want me to be

LIE

Why do we lie?

Thinking we

Are saving our own hide

Hoping that we

Can catch the tides

The one who loves you

Know that you have lied

You will Lie to show

You have a little pride

The one you love the most

Will accept that Lie

Still, they know

It is too deep

And it is too wide

Don't hurt the ones

Who love you the most

Remember, they will always

Give you a toast

One Lie will lead

Into another Lie

And lives are affected

By these great BIG LIES

CONNIE C. TOMLIN-VOGT

LOVE AND HAPPINESS

Is there Love And Happiness

When the voices start to rise

Let the silence step outside

Is there Love And Happiness

When a hug becomes a shove

Will the love turn on inside

Is there Love And Happiness

When a gentle touch

Becomes a fist with a punch

Someone has to quit

Yes,

There is Love And Happiness

When everyone keeps a level head

With an open mind and listen

To what is being felt

From the inside to the outside

Love and Happiness

Will not be denied

Connie C. Tomlin-Vogt

LOVE AND HATE

GOD'S Love,

Has more power

Over the Devil's Hate

GOD'S Love,

Will send you soul

To Heaven

The tranquil place

The Devil's Hate,

Will send your soul

To Hell

The heated place

GOD will teach us. Love

And not hate

Therefore, this earth can live

In this beautiful space

LOVE IS BLIND

Love Is Blind

Love is weak

Love should be given

To everyone that shall seek

Love Is Blind

Love is weak

Love should be given

To everyone at such a high peak

Love is Blind

Love is weak

Love should be given

To everyone that is meek

Love Is Blind

Love is weak

Love should be given

To everyone we meet

Connie C. Tomlin-Vogt

On the streets

LOVE IS JUST

Love Is Just, not one second

Love Is Just, not one minute

Love Is Just, not one hour

Love Is Just, not one day

Love Is Just, not one night

Love Is Just, not one week

Love Is Just, not one month

Love Is Just, not one year

Love is just, as the years grows near

Love is forever

That is infinity

This will keep

Us together

Through all types

Of weather

Connie C. Tomlin-Vogt

LOVE IS NOT A HOME

Love Is Not A Home

When that love is gone

Love Is Not A Home

When you are singing

The same old songs

Love Is Not A Home

When the laughter

Is put on hold

Love Is Not A Home

When the pain is

All so strong

Love In Not A Home

When two egos

Keep things going

And Knows right from wrong

LOVE IS...

Love Is joy

Love Is pain

Love Is like walking

In hot sand

Love Is gain

Love Is sane

Love Is like flames

Burning in the rain

Love Is peace

Love will not decease

Love will hold

Like pure gold

GOD only knows

Love plays a role

Connie C. Tomlin-Vogt

LOVE, DISCIPLINE AND SUPPORT

Love, Discipline And Support

Is what our little ones want
152

Love gives them character

Discipline tells them to say

I don't

Support the Parents

Who spank them

And do not give them

What they want

This will keep them

Within your hearts

Love, Discipline and Support

LOVE

Love is bitter

Love is sweet

Love is something

You can't beat

With the blazing

Hot heat

Love is bitter

Love is sweet

Love can make

You do things

That is

So, neat

Love is bitter

Love is sweet

Love will make you happy

And that's

A tasty treat

Connie C. Tomlin-Vogt

Love is bitter

Love is sweet

Love can make

You LOVE

This comes

Before Hate

MOTHER CAN BE

A Mother,

Is as caring

As can be

Just as delicate

As cotton balls

That is growing in

The cotton fields

She is sweet

As honey

That is made

From honeybees

Her love is deep

As the deep blue seas

Her heart

Will open wide

With anyone's keys

This is how

A Mother Can Be

Giving that Love

Connie C. Tomlin-Vogt

To you and me

CONNIE C. TOMLIN-VOGT

NOT A FRIEND

I need a friend

Not A Friend

Every now and then

I need a friend

Not A Friend

Whenever he or she can

I need a friend

Not A Friend

Who thinks him or her

Will never sin

I need a friend

Not A Friend

That does not

Take my hand

I need a friend

That can say

I will be here

Until the end

Because we are friends

This is who

You can call

A friend

NOTHING

If I could start

From Nothing again

What fun shall it be

I will make

The best of it

With lots of laughter

And without any pain

Keeping my head held high

GOD'S, guidance

I will regain

To get the needs

And not the wants

Will keep away

All aches and pain

The material things

Cannot help you maintain

It just brings on

A lot more

Agony and pain

Connie C. Tomlin-Vogt

LOVE, PEACE AND HAPPINESS

Is what keeps us

From going INSANE

160

PEOPLE

One thing

People should do

Is to let People

Live their lives, too

Without saying

"I do not like you",

Every one of us

Are here for a purpose

Like standing in line

To get pick

For the circus

So, please be kind

To everyone we meet

You will see yourself

Shining without defeat

POLITE

POLITE – NESS

Is due to everyone

Whether you are rich

Otherwise

Whether you are poor

Whether you are weak

Or whether you are strong

Whether you are smart

Or whether you are dumb

Whether you are here

Or whether you are there

Whether you are far

Or whether you are near

Just remember

Politeness is rated

As number one

POLITE – NESS

Is meant for everyone

REMEMBERING

Remembering the bad times

When you do not have a thin dime

Remembering the bad times

When the sun does not shine

Remembering the bad times

When you hear a wind chime

Remembering the bad times

When you cannot see a sign

Remembering the bad times

When you think

Everything is fine

Remembering the bad times

Will show time after time

So, stop

CONNIE C. TOMLIN-VOGT

And start thinking

About the good times

Keep that in mind

At all times

RESPECT

The Respect you have for others

You have learned something from

You're Father, Mother

Or anyone that Love ya,

The Respect you have for others

You can relate to a Sister

Or a Brother

Some of us have different

Father's and Mother's

The Respect you have for others

Is to Love one another

Shows you have been taught

By your Father and Mother

The Respect you have for others

Will carry you a lot more further

You have discovered this

Connie C. Tomlin-Vogt

From your Father and Mother

The Respect you have for others

Have Faith in him the Father

Look to be blessed by our

Glorious LORD and

Gracious GOD

Who is our Father

SO WIDE

The world

Is So Wide and deep

We do not know

Where to place our feet

Not knowing

The people

We will meet

Sitting by you

Or by me

In the next seat

Finding time

For a bite to eat

Chatting and smiling

To the same old beat

Thinking which one

Will stay a friend

And which one

Will try to flee

The world is

Connie C. Tomlin-Vogt

So Wide and so deep

Connie C. Tomlin-Vogt

STEREOTYPE

Stereotyping,

You did not learn

Nothing from your Mother

No one is better than the other

Look in the mirror at yourself

Not at your Sister or Brother

You should have learned not too

Stereotype from your Mother

To throw a rock and hide the hand

Make you look like a grain of sand

Love your neighbor as you love yourself

You should have learned not too

Stereotype from your mother

Criticizing others should not

Have been taught by your Mother

Accepting everyone's beautiful image

For whom they are, check yourself

Before you wreck yourself

This should have been taught

By your graceful and loving Mother

She did not try or even bother

Sent you into the world to judge others

You should have learn not to

Stereotype from your Mother

Stereotyping comes from lies, sin and shame

You caused it

So, you are the blame

Stop stereotyping and love one another

You should have learn not too

Stereotype from your Mother

STRONG

Offering me things

When you have done wrong

I will keep

My head held high

That is what

Makes me strong

I will take a deep breath

And keep dancing

To the same old songs

I will also keep my strength

To keep moving on

Never keeping this

A hush, hush situation

Because I am not going along

You are the one

Connie C. Tomlin-Vogt

That has made me strong

Now, let us both move on

172

THE GRANDPARENTS LOVE

The Grandparents Love,

Is the best love of all

When you hear

This tone of voice

It is the right call

The teaching

They teach

Will keep

You standing tall

Their knowledge

And understanding

Will not let us fall

The guidance

Will stop you

From running into

A brick wall

That is real love

The Grandparents Love

Connie C. Tomlin-Vogt

THE LAST DANCE

He ask her for a dance

Not knowing

That it would be

His friends' at his last dance

Being followed

For over fifteen miles

The drive by shooter's head

Must be in the clouds

To go home thinking

Nothing wrong was done

Are you going to be scorned?

For someone else, life is torn

This is what,

The Last Dance has done

All who were involved

Should realize

Innocent lives were ,involved too

A town and a county line

Were also driven through

Not giving respect

To another man, turf

What is this world coming too

Those weapons are not the support

We are going to fake

Taking a life

That you cannot make

We all should Love

And let go of the word Hate

TROOPS OF TWO-THOUSAND AND THREE (2003)

"FRONT LINE IS INFANTRY",

March, TROOPS OF TWO-THOUSAND AND THREE (2003)

The Iraqi Freedom War

Was about to begin

US Troops of women and men

Not knowing what to think

Packing their gears

However, never any fear

With their heads held high

For the ones who have lived

And the ones who have died

Family, friends and America too

Will forever be here for you

Right by your side, TROOPS

We want you to live

Instead of die

THANK YOU!

Because you have put

Your life on the line

We Love You,

Troops of Two-Thousand and Three (2003)

Americans are proud of all

Not just a few

Connie C. Tomlin-Vogt

WEAKER

It should always

Be fair and equal treatment

To all who are living

In these times and days

No one should be

At a suffering stage

A free meal

Only helps a little

Other necessary items

Would also help our needs

To live at a chance of living

We are getting

Weaker and Weaker

To call our self unique

Is only the environment

Saving our world from our own

Destruction, hate, racism,

Jealousy and outrageous deceit

Get wiser and stronger

Connie C. Tomlin-Vogt

Not Weaker and Weaker

Connie C. Tomlin-Vogt

WHERE THE LOVE HAS GONE

Where The Love Has Gone

Under the ground

Or dried up by the sun

Where The Love Has Gone

Out to sea

For no one to see

Where The Love Has Gone

When school is out

And there is nowhere to run

Where The Love Has Gone

Being sad will not

Make them come home

Where The Love Has Gone

The Devil has captured it

GOD is really the one

Where The Love Has Gone

JESUS has open arms

And anyone can come

Connie C. Tomlin-Vogt

WHO'S BUSINESS

There is this class

Who always

Keep their fingers

Stuck up their AH-CHOO

Always minding

Other folks business

Jacking their jaws

Not knowing what

They are talking about

Watching to see

If you are walking

With or without

Mind your own business

Try to become a friend

Will make you well known

Whose business it is

It is sure not yours

WHY

Why should I stand accused?

Why should I be misuse?

If I cannot stand

On my own two feet

Then, Why try

To knock me

Off my seat

I shall not

Be stand accuse

I do not try

To use or be misused

I do not want

To set off

Anyone's fuse

That is Why,

I will not

Be standing accuse

Connie C. Tomlin-Vogt

WIFE AND MOTHER

Life,

Is like a crossword puzzle

Being a Wife And Mother

Time after time

Doing for others

Giving love that goes unnoticed

Attention when things get bogus

Life,

Is like a crossword puzzle

Being a Wife And Mother

To put a smile on their face

With pride and not disgrace

Life,

Is like a crossword puzzle

Being a Wife And Mother

Open communications

Have no exceptions to the game

Life,

Is like a crossword puzzle

Being a Wife And Mother

Doing things that should be done

Listening to everyone's view

Keeping the family together

And all its values true

WITH HOPE THERE MAY BE LOVE

With Hope,

There May Be Love

Keeping our heads together

So, our love will prolong

With Hope,

There May Be Love

Keeping our heads together

Therefore, nothing will go wrong

With Hope,

There May Be Love

Keeping our heads together

So we can dance

By the tune alone

With Hope,

There May Be Love

Keeping our heads together

Therefore, things will be

In the right time zone

With Hope,

There May Be Love

Keeping our heads together

Make us keep the right tone

We can all sing along

With Hope, There May Be Love

Summary

Love And Hate This Life is showing Love to everyone that we may encounter, because all of us have feelings. When someone else's feelings are not considered, never show any hatred. The respect that you had for yourself and for him or her is all gone to pieces. Love all, no matter who, what or where he or she came from. Love him or her as you would love yourself this world will become a more beautifully, beautiful and Loving, not a Hating place. Share the Love, and you will receive the Love more than a million times. ***CCTV***

BOOK 3

LIVING AS WE GROW STRONG

A Message To My Readers

To my Readers, Living As We Grow Strong is to lend a helping hand to anyone that is in need of one. To lift a person's spirits when they are down will bring on a little smile. We can also leave the past behind us, stay with the present and look forward to a bright future. Each dark road that is taken, a light has to be at the end of it. Taking a step each day, this helps us to grow stronger and wiser, not weaker. *CCTV*

A CHANCE TO GROW

To the Child that did not give

Themselves A Chance To Grow

Slow down to let Mom and Dad know

On showing you

How to make that dough

When it is time for you to mow

You will be dazzling

From head to toe

Children, give yourself time to sew

Then plant that seed

And watch it grow

Children give yourself

A Chance To Grow

And things will flow as you go

Connie C. Tomlin-Vogt

A MARRIED MAN

Little Sister, Little Sister

What are you doing?

Having a child from A Married Man

Is not something

That you want to do

Little Sister, Little Sister

What are you doing?

Threaten to call his wife

Because things are not

Working out for you

Little Sister, Little Sister

What are you doing?

A Married Man who has a family

And he is not going

To leave them for you

Little Sister, Little Sister

What are you doing?

Making you look bad

And other women, too

Little Sister, Little Sister

Find yourself a single man

So, that our family values

Will stay true, Little Sister

A Married Man will not do

A PRECIOUS JEWEL

Your body is like

A Precious Jewel

Don't let anyone use it

Like it is a tool

Your body is like

A Precious Jewel

Don't let anyone touch it

As if it was cool

Your body is like

A Precious Jewel

Don't let anyone see it

As if they were reading

A book from school

Your body is like

A Precious Jewel

Don't let anyone hunger for it

As if it was a piece of food

Your body is like A Precious Jewel

Connie C. Tomlin-Vogt

ABSTINENCE

Abstinence,

Is what we preach

To teach

Our children sex

Is not exactly

What they should seek

Speak the right thing

To them

Not to have sex

Before marriage

We will not see them

With a baby carriage

ADULTS

Adults get a grip

And pick up that

Good old switch

Show our children

Who is in charge

Let them know

You have put

Up your guards

They will push

To see how far

They can go

Put the petal

To the floor

It can flow

We all must glow

Connie C. Tomlin-Vogt

BEING THE NEW KID

Being The New Kid on the block,

That clock just doesn't

Tick tock

Being The New Kid on the block,

It's like wearing a hole

In your socks

Being The New Kid on the block,

Is going fishing alone

Off the wooden docks

Being The New Kid on the block,

Sometimes act dumb

Instead of smart

Being The New Kid on the block

Try not to put your foot

In your mouth

Connie C. Tomlin-Vogt

Being The New Kid on the block

Speak when spoken too

And always knock

Connie C. Tomlin-Vogt

CHILDREN OF TODAY

Children Of Today,

Do not know

What is headed their way

Children Of Today

May have it harder

Day to day

Children Of Today

Want the sun to shine

And the rain to go away

Children Of Today

Some want to fight

And some want to play

Children Of Today

Some Mothers

Take up for them

And not knowing

What they have done

Children Of Today

Take each day

Systematically

And live each day

Day by day

Connie C. Tomlin-Vogt

DAUGHTERS ARE...

A Daughter Love

Daughters Are precise

Daughters Are priceless

With lots of hugging,

Kissing and sharing

Daughters are precious

Daughters are sweet

Daughters are love

That just can't be beat

Daughters are joy

Daughters are happiness

Daughters are pure

So, Mothers

Please make sure

Daughters are a gift

That money can't buy

So, Daughters

Help Mom and Dad

To stay alive

And not live a lie

Connie C. Tomlin-Vogt

DAWN TO DUSK

The day begins

Dawn To Dusk

Children are already

Talking, playing

And clowning around

Without a rush

Dusk is here

Settling down is a must

The early night hours

Time to lie down

The children are still

Smiling, laughing,

And horse playing around

Nine-fifteen is now bedtime

Climbing into bed

Putting up a little fuss

Within thirty minutes

Bedtime is what we trust

Fast asleep

CONNIE C. TOMLIN-VOGT

Dreaming and wishing

For dawn again

A new day will start

And the fun begins

From dawn to dusk again

DISRESPECTFUL SON

These so-called Parents

Who has a disrespectful Son

Going around breaking up families

That tries to keep a happy home

When they see him as a freak

To disrespect you as his Parents

And he himself, too

The teaching you gave

To him, as a child

He will go out into the world

And not make you proud

That family will say,

"What kind of Parents are they?"

To know that they're Son

Is out in the streets

Provoking a family with deceit

His family says,

"That family is ignorant,

For acting that way"

He should have been taught

To have respect for others

If they have respect, too

What kind of Fathers

And Mothers, are you

Not teaching your son

How to respect others

Fathers and Mothers, too

Connie C. Tomlin-Vogt

DON'T EVER KNOCK A MAN

Don't ever knock a man

For what he does

He is using the gift

God has sent him from above

Don't ever knock a man

For what he does

One day, you might need him

To give you some love

Don't ever knock a man

For what he does

If he cannot be there for you

One day, he will come through

Don't ever knock a man

For what he does

We are equal to each other

If we are only zero feet tall

Connie C. Tomlin-Vogt

Don't ever knock a man

For What He Does

FAMILY

Family,

Is the greatest

Source under the Sun

When you consider

Yourself as one

The fun has just begun

Showing the love

You have for one another

Will make closer

Sisters and Brothers

Family is number one

Helping each other grow

To stay stronger

While living life longer

FATHERS

Fathers are special

Just as special as can be

Giving us love

Like we want it to be

Fathers can make

Sour things taste very sweet

Making sure whenever we meet

He will always have a tasty treat

Fathers know-how

To be kind

Keeping our pockets

Fill with nickels and dimes

Knowing we all will be on time

For each and every one

Of those nickels and dimes

CONNIE C. TOMLIN-VOGT

GRANDFATHERS

Grandfathers

The one

Who will be there

Giving us love

No one can make

Laughs and smiles

Like baking a cake

Grandfathers see

How many generations to be

Capturing the love

Between the ones he sees

Making sure

The day goes right

Hence be able

To sleep tight at night

A Grandfathers Love

The best Love ever

Cause things to be safer

For his children

And his future generations

Will live forever and ever

Connie C. Tomlin-Vogt

HAVE WE OVERCOME

Have We Overcome?

The race has started

And never won

Have We Overcome?

The dawn of a new day

Brings brightness

From the indoor Sun

Have We Overcome?

All that our eyes

Can only see

Are colors in the light

Have We Overcome?

Will I be shelter from the rain?

With a torn hat

Or a home

Have we ever or will we ever overcome?

Have We Overcome?

Connie C. Tomlin-Vogt

HIT AND RUN

I was hit

By a

Hit And Run

The children

They were all so stun

Not knowing the one

Who did the Hit And Run

Telling is like

Lying in the hot sun

No smile or laughter

And not any fun

This lets us know

GOD is still

Running the show

Because the Devil is busy

In all towns and cities

While catching his prey

Along the way

I was hit

Connie C. Tomlin-Vogt

By a Hit And Run

Connie C. Tomlin-Vogt

HIT FROM BEHIND

When a human

Hit you from behind

They are coward

In everyone's mind

Also not human enough

To stand face to face

They will cheat, lie

And try to win the race

Not thinking

About the case

Being a hot-head

Will leave

A bitter taste

Knowing that you

Have just lost

A loosing race

When you have been

Hit from behind

And not standing

Face to face

All cowards

Will see this

On Judgment Day

CONNIE C. TOMLIN-VOGT

I KNOW YOU HAVE DONE IT

I Know You Have Done It

To me again

With a silly smile

A so call pretty little grin

I Know You Have Done It

To me again

You think you are smart

Yet you are not going to win

I Know You Have Done It

To me again

Taking the food out of my mouth

And my next of kin

I Know You Have Done It

To me again

You don't care

If I am living in something

That is made out of tin

I Know You Have Done It

To me again

Laughing like life is a game for me

But that will not make me bend

I Know You Have Done It

To me again

And you know this is a sin

A trip to hell is what you have won

I Know You Have Done It

To me again

Jesus is my Savior

And my Faith is in Him

You have done it to me again

Connie C. Tomlin-Vogt

IF YOU DON'T

If You Don't want

You're Mother, Father,

Sister or Brother

Done like that

Why are you stabbing?

Others in the back

If You Don't want

You're Grandmother, Grandfather,

Grandaunt or Granduncle

Done like that

Why are you judging others?

They are also a part of the pack

If You Don't want

You're Aunt, Uncle

Or Cousin

Done like that

Then place yourself

On that rack

If You Don't want

You're Wife, Husband,

Son or Daughter

Done like that

Why do others have to

Put up with your slack

If You Don't want

Anyone You know

Done like that

Then keep your favors

In your sack

Connie C. Tomlin-Vogt

INFLUENCE

Being Influenced by someone else,

Hurts the one who loves you

The most and best

Being Influence by someone else,

Destroys your mind

And put you through a test

Being Influenced by someone else,

Cause the family a lot of

Heartaches and stress

Being Influenced by someone else,

Who doesn't care less

Will make you obsessed

Being Influence by someone

Keep things positive and move on

And leave the negative things alone

Being Influenced by someone else,

Who gives you guidance

Tell you nothing wrong

Stand beside you

To make sure you stay all

So mighty strong

Not weak and especially not torn

INVASIONS

Invasions of others privacy

When it is not needed

Peace is what we want

No killing, and please, no hate

We all should have Faith

Invasions of others privacy

When it is not needed

Peace is what we want

Not mass graves

We all should be save

Invasions of others privacy

When it is not needed

Peace is what we want

Stop hiding in caves

Like, you are all so brave

Invasions of others privacy

When it is not needed

Peace is what we want

Know when to vacate

The innocent are dying

Countries are crying

Peace is what we want

And we want it to cease today

Connie C. Tomlin-Vogt

IT'S ALL ABOUT HIM

There are men

Who thinks It's All About Him

Running your woman away

That will make her astray

There are men

Who think It's All About Him

Having a good woman

Who will try to stay

There are men

Who think It's All About Him

Being a man is listening

To what she has to say

There are men

Who think It's All About Him

Doing things that are ugly

Instead of keeping things lovely

There are men

Who think It's All About Him

Telling you what you want to hear

Therefore, he can make you steer

There are men

Who think It's All About Him

Chasing other women in the streets

He should only be thinking about

Being discreet

Connie C. Tomlin-Vogt

MOTHERS TO DAUGHTERS

Mothers should keep things

Open to Daughters

Allow them to speak

From the heart

Listen to what they are saying

And be that special part

Daughters are like

The petal of a red rose

With the actions they give

No one knows

Those moments

Should be there

To hear the saying

Of a Mothers prayer

Daughters are nice

Daughters are neat

Daughters are sweet

I pray to you, LORD

So they will receive

Many treats

235

Daughters should obey

And keep out of trouble

For the loving and kindness

Of their dear and lovely Mother

From Mothers To Daughters

NO HAND LAND

The system

Of the No Hand Land

Will not give you

Mud made from sand

The only thing

It wants to do

Is play in the sun and tan

To take all that it can

The hand of the No Man Land

It wants to see you

Without nothing

Left in the pan

The hand of the No Man Land

Will never

Because it can

The failing system

Of the

No Hand Land

NO ONE

Who will give help when it is needed?

NO ONE!

When hands

Were held out

God made sure

They were filled

You try to pretend

My hands

Would be filled

When I needed you

However, you were

Never there

That showed me

You did not care

The time will come

Both hands are filled

Then we can keep

Connie C. Tomlin-Vogt

All things at will

NOT

Being poor

Is NOT that bad

Not having

The things you need

Is what

Makes us sad

NOT Shelter,

NOT Electric,

NOT Heat

And sometimes

NOT any food to eat

Helping those

Who are poor

Will let us know

We are at the core

And we can start

With a flow

OPINION

Everyone has

Their own Opinion

Listening and understanding

Is what counts

If you don't want

To hear the response

Of someone else

Then, keep the matter

To yourself

Try not to say,

"You think you know everything"

Just sit and listen

To what is about to be said

Show them you can refrain

PROBLEMS

If Problems

Are so hard to solve

Give those

Who are willing

The chance

To solve them

For us all

Face up

To the fact

That one man

Do not know everything

Giving unjust Judgments'

Thinking that

You are better

Because the Problems

You have

Is a game of shame

That is the signature

You sign as

Your name

QUICK TO JUDGE

Everyone is so quick to judge

Sometimes you hurt others

Try not to work so fast

Everyone is so quick to judge

The looking glass

Will never forget the past

Everyone is so quick to judge

The crystal ball gets cloudy

When you put others last

Everyone is so quick to judge

If you judge others

You are no better than another

Everyone is so quick to judge

Always look

In the looking glass first

Connie C. Tomlin-Vogt

And this will

Quench one's thirst

CONNIE C. TOMLIN-VOGT

RELEASE THE PEACE

Release the peace

All over the World

Release the Peace

To every boy and girl

Release the peace

That is what

We should speak

Release the peace

To lay your weapons

In the streets

Release the peace

To bring all wars

To an end

Release the peace

Connie C. Tomlin-Vogt

Stop the killings

Of our men

Release the peace

And stop saying you

Do not know when

Release the peace

We all have sin

Over and over again

SECURITY

Security

Brings on trust

Security

Brings on peace

Security

Brings on unity

If life

Had security for all

This world

Would start to spin

Like a spinning ball

It takes away the hardship

Leave good memories, too

Will also aid

Within our body and soul

To help us renew

Connie C. Tomlin-Vogt

Security can make you feel

Like life

Is peacefully real

Security can make you feel

Like life

Is peacefully real

248

SEE, DRINK AND BY GRAB DON'T TELL ALL

See All,

To see

All you can see

Sometimes the eyes

And the mind

Will play tricks on you

Whatever the mind thinks

Maybe totally different

From what the eyes see

Drink All,

To Drink All

You can drink

Make sure to carry all you can

Inside of your stomach

Not a bit more

Never put your cup down

Once you have crossed anyone's door

Connie C. Tomlin-Vogt

And By, Grab Don't Tell All

Whatever you here

Never repeat it to anyone

Lives of others are involved

Unless it is a matter

Of life or death

You can tell some, none

Or you can Tell All

Connie C. Tomlin-Vogt

SELL OUT

Sell Out your value

For that dollar

Will make any human

Scream and holler

Sell Out your value

For that dollar

How can you step so low

Sell Out your value

For that dollar

Everyone will take a blow

Sell Out your value

For that dollar

Now, no man can watch

The show

Sell Out your value

Connie C. Tomlin-Vogt

For that dollar

How do you expect

Your own to grow

252

Sell Out your value

For that dollar

Being greedy

Is all that you know

To Sell Out the value

Of that dollar

Take a swallow

There is no time

To follow

SOUL

Soul,

Will be with you

When things

Are turning to rust

Soul,

Will see you

For the just

And the unjust

Soul,

Will show comfort

In the time of need

That is a must

Soul,

Will be there

For the previous and latest

Without a ruckus

Connie C. Tomlin-Vogt

Soul,

Is here to be with you

From the highest mountain

To the lowest

Depth of the deep blue seas

Soul,

Is to the bone

It carries

An even greater zone

This allows us

To build a better home

CONNIE C. TOMLIN-VOGT

STOP WITH THE MADNESS

The suffering

Has to

Stop With The Madness

The rich is getting richer

The poor is getting poorer

The knowledge

We should share

The kindness

Of how much we care

The storm is raging

The hate is degrading

The star will shine

In all due time

The LORD will say,

"That you are Bless mankind"

Connie C. Tomlin-Vogt

TALK ABOUT ME

Talk About Me

Behind my back

Be sure you have

The right facts

Talk About Me

Behind my back

I will not give you

Any slack

Talk About Me

Behind my back

I am sure you are trying

To peak through the cracks

Talk About Me

Behind my back

I maybe bless

With an unknown request

Talk About Me

Behind my back

Time is flying

So, get on the right track

Talk About Me

Behind my back

Sweep around your own door

You will not get an attack

This is a known fact

Talk to me to my face

I will help you

Face to face

Then, we will be

On the same pace

Connie C. Tomlin-Vogt

TEACH MY SON

Teach My Son

How to be a man

And appreciate the woman

At his hand

Teach My Son

How to be a man

And appreciate the woman

Who will stick by him

Through thick and thin

Teach My Son

How to be a man

And appreciate the woman

Who accepts him as her man

Teach My son

How to be a man

To give respect with Love

And be the best Gentleman

That he can

I am teaching my son

How to be a man

Because he is a great man

This will make any woman

Take his hand

Connie C. Tomlin-Vogt

THE 90's MOM

A Mother of the 90's

Is different from the 80's

The children of today

Attitudes are just

A little shady

Children do not care

Meanwhile, mothers are there

Willing and able to see

Her little ones

Learn to share

Listen with

A listening ear

Mother is such a dear

They will make sure

Your life

Will not disappear

So, keep both

Compassion and mentality

Close and clear

For The 90's, MOM

Is so near

Connie C. Tomlin-Vogt

THE BEST LEADERS

The Best Leaders

Are the one

That is there

The most

Just keep

Things rolling

While you stand

At your post

Don't catch

The wrong ride

Just stay on the coast

And do not forget

About that boasts

Those are

The Best Leaders

That will give you a toast

CONNIE C. TOMLIN-VOGT

THE CHILDREN OF THE WORLD

We are

The Children Of The World

Want to live

Safe from destruction

Sharing the same feelings

Will make us as one

You can Love or Hate

To keep it under cover

You should

Always participate

The Children Of The World

This is for every

Boy and girl

That is a part of this

Whole Wide World

Connie C. Tomlin-Vogt

THE COST OF FREEDOM
MONEY,

Why does it take you to run the entire world?

These big boilers shot callers

Sitting back in their rooms

Around their tables

Or at their desks

With their pencils, pens and papers

Others who have worked

So hard in building

One of the richest

Countries in the World,

Excuses are The Cost Of Freedom

Who has freedom?

Some can steal, murder

And do whatever they want, too

Just to get a slap

On the back of their hands

While some who cannot afford

Anything and living in poverty

Because of The Cost Of Freedom

Still, yet, we are one of the

Wealthiest Country in the World

Calling ourselves the wisest

Nevertheless, are we the dumbest?

With an unbalance environment

"We Shall Never Rise",

And "Never Overcome" from

The Cost Of Freedom

Remember, America is number one

And we take care of our own

THE ENEMY

What if you were they and you were The Enemy?

What would you do?

How will you solve the problem?

How long will it take to solve the problem?

Is there a problem with them?

Is there a problem with you?

Or maybe there is a problem with me?

Make sure that the problem

With the enemy

Is not looking in the mirror

In front of you

This is where

All our problems come true

It is always looking

And staring at you

THE HAPPY HOME

Infidelity,

With someone else spouse

You are tearing up

Their home

And your house

If you think

This is good

You have been

Misunderstood

Two times two

Equals four

Nosey your way

Out of their door

Putting someone

Through a scandal

Is that

Really your handle

Walking back and forth

In their footsteps

Connie C. Tomlin-Vogt

Do you need some help?

Carrying on and on and on

See you both

Have broken up

A beautiful

And The Happy Home

Not caring about

What he or she

Has done

With or without

Tearing up

The Happy Home

YOU THINK YOU ARE BETTER

You Think You Are Better

You lied on the innocent

You are rotten to the core as ever

You Think You Are Better

Going around lying on the innocent

When you are sleeping with the devil

You Think You Are Better

The lies you have told on the innocent

Lands like a plucked chicken feather

You Think You Are Better

While telling lies on the innocent

The relationship will change like the weather

You Think You Are Better

Still telling lies on the innocent

Buying Love instead of earning Love

Connie C. Tomlin-Vogt

You should hesitate

You Think You Are Better

From lies you have told on the innocent

You keep your nose

In everyone's else business

Instead of tending to your own

You Think You Are Better

Still lying on the innocent

Wanting people to see others

Through your eyes

When you do not care for me

How do you know if I care for you

You Think you Are Better

The lies that you have told on the innocent

Will never get you into Heaven

However, your BODY, MIND and SOUL

Are doomed for 7734

Better known as HELL turned upside down

CONNIE C. TOMLIN-VOGT

THE NICE GUY

Being The Nice Guy

Always makes you cry

The pain that it brings

Is like listening

To the horn of a freight train

Before it is about to rain

When you think

Things are about to change

Another big smack in the face

Puts you back in chains

Never to know if things

Will ever get better

Praying to our Savior

Who sends all types of weather

Realizing now that things

Will never get better

Connie C. Tomlin-Vogt

For The Nice Guy

Only the seasons

Changes the weather

THE ROCK

The Diamond in The Rock

Is a very precious jewel

Do not chisel

The wrong way

It can chip

You're stone

With the tool

Hold it up

To the sky

Watch it sparkle

With your eyes

The most beautiful

Stone of all

Is like the waters

Glittering from a waterfall

With that Diamond

Shining bright

You may not need much light

Family should be there

Connie C. Tomlin-Vogt

Both day and night together

THE VIOLENCE

If there is Violence

In the School House

Then, the Parents

Should do better teaching

And nosing around

In their own house

Our Students are killing

Students and Teachers

This is not right

Hitting the Teacher

In the head with a hammer

Things have gone

Out of sight

The ones

Who are doing right

Do suffer

Because of the ones

Who wants to fight

Families pulling together

CONNIE C. TOMLIN-VOGT

Will pay a big

And important price

We need to stop

The Violence

CONNIE C. TOMLIN-VOGT

TIME HAS GONE

Sitting here

As the day

Goes by

Watching the clouds

Dance in the sky

Now the time

Has gone

The wind

Gets strong

The rain

Begins to fall

The lightning flashes

And the thunder

Started to roll

This is

A terrible storm

With a glare

In our eyes

And fear

Connie C. Tomlin-Vogt

In our hearts

Make this storm

Simple and short

As they come

TIME WILL TELL

Time Will Tell

If the right things

Were done

You have wondered

If you have

Done anything wrong

Put it in a question

To ask oneself

To see how things

Are coming along

You may also

Want to be alone

If so, try to do

What is right

Not anything

That is wrong

Love your

Brothers and sisters

For they should not

Lead you on

Keep each other happy

Because family

And friends

Do not lean

However, must

Stand strong

Please make this

An eccentric home

USE ME

Use Me,

For whatever

You can

Use Me,

If there is

Not a band

Use Me,

If you cannot

Even stand

Use Me,

If you have

To sit

In the sand

Use Me,

Because I have

Connie C. Tomlin-Vogt

A darker tan

Use Me,

I will lend you a hand

If you call

I will be here, there

And everywhere

So, Use Me

For whatever

Reason you can

Not because you can

WAR

Going off to War

Is a great chore

We want it to be

An even score

Fighting and killing

Each other

Is like a bad sore

Making and keeping

The PEACE

Will make us soar

Standing on a platform

To decide

No War, no more

We would like

PEACE

To come

Behind open

And close doors

No more WAR

Summary

Living As We Grow Strong, this world should never be divided by any kind of source whatsoever. Our nation is a nation of one, to let a few who have helped themselves and the many that have conquered by helping them. Everyone deserves an opportunity to grow to the fullest during his or her natural life. The self-indulgence that some of us have and not sharing the generosity to others who made you who you are. This is a shame on us as a nation that does not give ourselves an option to live and grow strong. ***CCTV***

About the Author

Connie Cecelia Tomlin-Vogt, Born in Philadelphia, Pennsylvania on February 11, 1963 and grew up in Sumter, South Carolina. I attended the public schools and Morris College both in Sumter, South Carolina. After leaving Morris College, I was married and we resided in Charleston, South Carolina for ten years, three years were for military purposes. We have six children and eight grandchildren presently. We relocated to Greenville, South Carolina, living here for the past thirty plus years. I enrolled as a student at ITT Technical Institute, Greenville, South Carolina March 2011 until March 2015. Graduated April 2015 with a Bachelor of Science Degree. Taking the time out while working, I also helped take care of my Disable Love Ones 2016-2023. PRAYERS and finding the time with all the research of not giving up on my POETRY Work and Self-Publishing. I was BLESSED to have found an Awesome Company to help me Publish my Writings and this is where my journey begins at becoming a Self-Publish Author. Thanks to my BFF SB who motivated me the most and to the team of Professionals at Spines Publishing Company for such an Awesome Job in making a Dream come True. poetryliriksbyctv@gmail.com
CCTV

www.ingramcontent.com/pod-product-compliance
Lightning Source LLC
Chambersburg PA
CBHW070747160726
48004CB00001B/89